Love & Sambal

LOVE & SAMBAL

Poems

Jeddie Sophronius

THE WORD WORKS
WASHINGTON, D.C.

Love & Sambal © 2024 Jeddie Sophronius

Reproduction
of this book in any form
or by any means, electronic
or mechanical, except when quoted
in part for the purpose of review,
must be with permission in
writing from the publisher.
Address inquiries to
THE WORD WORKS

P.O. Box 42164
Washington, DC 20015
editor@wordworksbooks.org

Author photograph: Aubrey Carely
Cover design: Susan Pearce
Interior design: Emma Berver

ISBN: 978-1-944585-78-5
LCCN: 2023944875

Acknowledgments

An abundance of gratitude to the editors of the following publications where these poems first appeared, sometimes in earlier forms:

About Place Journal: "City of Flames"
Buah zine: "Love & Sambal"
The Cincinnati Review: "Swamp"
diaCRITICS: "City of Flood"
the minnesota review: "City of Smoke" and "Chinezenmoord"
The Nasiona: "Self-Portrait as a Failed Chinese Lover"
Prospectus: "Mother's Survival Notes"
Redivider: "Ganyang Cina"
Relief: A Journal of Art and Faith: "The Dying of the Chinese in Me"
River Styx: "Aftertaste"
The Roadrunner Review: "Where a Name Is Buried"
Sheila-Na-Gig online: "Reminiscence"
SHIFT: A Publication of MTSU Write: "Flood Ghazal" and "Overflow"
Sixfold: "I Rest My Mother Tongue"
Touchstone Literary Magazine: "Visitor"
Vinyl: "Rafflesia"
Watershed Review: "Altar"

"Porridge" was anthologized in *The Flavors of Home, a Pamlico Writer's Anthology*. "In the Waves of Midnight" was anthologized in *Mingled Voices 3*, the 2018 Proverse Poetry Prize Anthology. "Swamp" was anthologized in *Best Spiritual Literature* (formerly *The Orison Anthology*) Vol. 5, 2020.

Great admiration and appreciation to the Chinese-Indonesian writers and artists who waded through the swamp of our history, whose work paved the path for many others, including myself.

I am forever grateful to Western Michigan University, the University of Virginia, and The Speakeasy Project, for their continuous support. To my early poetry mentors, Nancy Eimers, Robert Evory, Paige Lewis, Sara Lupita Olivares, Emily O'Neill, and John Withee, for showing me the way. Special thanks to S. Marie Lafata-Clay, who convinced me to switch to poetry in one cold spring semester. To my biggest supporter and wisest teacher, Becky Cooper, for believing in me when I did not believe in myself. To the brilliant teachers at UVA's MFA program: Rita Dove, Debra Nystrom, Kiki Petrosino, Lisa Russ Spaar, and Brian Teare. Their words and guidance shaped me who I am today. To James Livingood and Barbara Moriarty, for making the program a home. To my cohort, Hodges Adams, Hannah Dierdorff, Kyle Marbut, and Raisa Tolchinsky, for the memories, laughs, and bottomless drinks. To my colleagues, Katie Airy, Hajjar Baban, Helena Chung, Aliyah Cotton, Michelle Gottschlich, for the love and secrets we've shared. Thank you to all my students for their trust, hope, and cheers. All the encouragement and generosity I have received from everyone mentioned made this book possible. I am forever indebted.

My deepest gratitude to The Word Works team for making my book dream come true, especially to Nancy White, whose wisdom and care flow through her words. I cannot thank you all enough.

To my companions in Indonesia, past and present, for our shared experiences that fuel my poems and made me the person I am today: Arvy Aulia, Vika Damay, Audrey Gracia Muljono, Elvira Benita Panggabean, Adinda Vashti Raissa, Ezekiel Ray, Nadia Niserena Pricillia Rimbing, Thea Samantha, Gabriel Sutanto, Ezra Putranto Wahyudi, and Tio Wijaya. To my confidantes, Ferena Debineva, Anindya Meidriani, and Prameswari Noor, for your precious presence and words. To my fellow international friends in Charlottesville, Vinton Cheng, Kyaw Moe Khine, Ihuoma Njoku, and Jinchao Zhao, for bringing home closer to all of us.

To Jayanto Tan for permission to use his art and for continuing to inspire me. To my closest friend and the first-reader of every single one of my poems, Nadia Karenina, for everything. Terima kasih semuanya. Lastly, shoutout to my family for their spiritual support and entrusting me with the freedom to walk my own, unprofitable, and rebellious path: my mother, Julia Suleeman, my sister, Elita Jessamine, my father, Robby Chandra, and my brother, Arvin Nathanael. To my faithful companion, Caviar, for keeping me company during my late-night hours for over a decade.

And finally, a timeless gratitude to 我的爱, Jingrun Lin. You are God-sent. Here's to us.

Contents

Porridge / 3

I

City of Flames / 7
Certificate of Citizenship / 9
Mother's Survival Notes / 11
The Dying of the Chinese in Me / 12
Elegy for My Grandfather / 13
May, 1998 / 14
Lunch With My Mother at a Restaurant / 16
Swamp / 18
Ode to the Activists / 19
Sestina / 20
Visitor / 22
Altar / 24

II

City of Flood / 27
Dear Indonesia / 30
Overflow / 32
Rafflesia / 33
Cina Komunis / 34
Flood Ghazal / 35
Ganyang Cina / 36
Cina / 37
In the Waves of Midnight / 38

III

    City of Concrete / 43
    Dutch East Indies / 44
    Chinezenmoord / 46
    Where a Name Is Buried / 48
    Ancestral Burden / 50

IV

    City of Smoke / 53
    Missing / 55
    Notations on Letting Go / 56
    Love & Sambal / 58
    Aftertaste / 59
    Reflections of a Failed Chinese Lover / 60
    Reminiscence / 61
    I Rest My Mother Tongue / 62
    Monsoon Elegy / 63

Coda: Present Day / 67

Notes / 83
About the Author / 85
About The Word Works / 85
Other Word Works Books / 86

For my ancestors

Porridge

There is sorrow in the eyes
of a cow, oceans hidden beneath flesh,
waiting to be calmed by a single prayer.

Sometimes I wonder why my body
is not my body, why this suffering
is not my suffering, but a door to a place
I otherwise will not remember.

Once, a mother sat and watched
her son eat leftover porridge for dinner.
Take my portion, she said. And he did.

I

I daily face,
this immigrant,
this man with my own face.

—Li-Young Lee

City of Flames

> *October 8, 2020: Over 400 people arrested in the capital after protesting against the dubious Job Creation Act, believed to harm workers' rights, among others.'*

No sparrows today. The air
        smells like burnt cockroaches.

My father is watching the news:
        Jakarta burned through the night.

Water cannons, tear gas, police
        in riot gear, wave after wave

of bodies crashing. The masses
        losing their numbers, shouts

morphing into screams. I see
        a picture on my phone:

one protestor embracing
        a policeman, the sky

clouded with smoke. Yesterday,
        I didn't leave the house,

afraid of being arrested
        or bringing trouble to my

family. Truly, it's my father
        I worry about, the things

I might bring back from his
            memory. Every protest,

he forbids his children
            from joining. His sister

fell during a riot twelve
            years ago and never

woke up. I'm failing as
            a minority in this country,

falling slowly as raindrops
            from a burning tree.

Certificate of Citizenship

My mother delivered me
to this land, her ancestral tears
washed me clean after my first cry.

I am the son of tidal waves and love,
bodies crashing under clouded skies.
As a child, I kissed the mango

tree in my backyard, traced fingers
along the moss growing on warm
stone fences. Down to my shoulders,

my hair flew with me wherever:
rocky hills, rice fields, or muddy
streets. The other boys teased me, called

me a girl, called me pretty. Once
the ice cream peddler arrived
with his box of fruit popsicles,

we piled around him, forgave one
another, then looked for a spot
to squat on the street, where our elbows

could rest against our knees. Fingers
turned sweet with the melted cream.
Tio, the oldest among them said,

Stop slouching, puff your chest.
He was my first friend. By the time
we heard the call to prayer,

we were already home. I have more
stories to tell, testimonies
of my childhood: like how I got lost

and mistook someone else's
country for my own.

Mother's Survival Notes

Let the night hide the color of your skin,
the contours of your eyes, the dragon
in your tongue.

        Even better if you don't walk at night.

Don't iron your shirt. Wear your crease, show
how poor you are. If you had money, you
wouldn't be walking.

        Don't walk like a sissy. And build those muscles.

Avoid taking the bus at night, unless
your feet are burning.
Even then, keep walking.

        Pray before leaving the house.

The people in this country murdered
your grandfathers in daylight. They didn't
fight back.

        Even better if you don't leave the house.

You are not one of them. Don't
let them know. If a stranger
asks your name, lie. Always lie.

The Dying of the Chinese in Me

The Chinese boy in me was killed when the authorities
forced my mother to change her name under a pear tree.
Little girls with almond eyes couldn't walk the streets
for anything: a pack of cigarettes, a bag of ginseng tea.

When I think of my father, who doesn't speak
with the tongue of a snake, I see how lucky he is:
people ignored the Chinese in him. Tio asked,
"Why do your kind say *I* differently than mine?" I sipped

my tea, avoided his gaze. I know: our mothers stand
under umbrellas and wait for their sons to return;
our sisters live in hiding, looking out their windows,
their tears can't wash away the street names; schools,

stores, our grandfathers burned or hanged on a pole.
Was it not enough when we cut the braids from our heads?
Under burning sky lanterns, a grandfather's hands fold,
a tulip on his chest, lips chanting something Chinese.

Elegy for My Grandfather

I never knew how you died, only remembered it happened
days or weeks after Grandma's death. The hospital,

the morgue, my dream of seeing your body
suspended in air, your funeral—I was too young

to cry. Was I three or five? You taught me chess
before I could speak, I replaced my king with a robot toy

half the size of the board. You didn't protest. You never did
talk much, let your laughs do the talking. Those quiet

moments, the two of us staring at black and white pieces.
Did you gasp for air? Did you tell your children you love them?

One morning I woke up, my mother told me to wear black,
the rest, fragments. Uncle—the son you disgraced—

carrying me as I tried to recognize the person in the casket.
I shunned the face, out of fear it might

be you, that you might visit me in dreams.
I stared at the lilies and gladiolas instead, scattered

over your red tie, chest, white-gloved hands, legs.
It was a strange way for the adults to say they'll miss you,

each of them standing tall, silent—like willows
surrounding my small body.

May, 1998

I was a child
    abandoned in the riots.
My family hid in the mountains.

    I hid at home. I'm trying
to catalog the incompleteness
    in my memory: rice and eggs

for a week; the rifle under a soldier's arm,
    signaling my caretaker and I
to turn the other way; *we're out*

    of rice, she said; the flea market
deserted; the rioters passing us,
    spinning their shirts

above their heads; a hint of smoke
    in the air; the walk
home, the house, the street,

    my heartbeat—
so quiet. Today, I am he
    speaking broken Indonesian.

What I have left
    of my country remains
forever incomplete. I've seen

    the crowded refugee boats,
trailing toward dim-lit land.
    Tonight, I am the guilty sea

that carried my ancestors here.
    Tonight, I am my sister's tomb,
the consuming flame, the crowd

    that watches, and the hum
of torches. In the end, we
    are the sacrifice.

What do we do with all this, burning?

Lunch With My Mother at a Restaurant

Kalambaka, Greece, 2008

From there, I could see the old, fallen
meteor and the monastery on its peak.

*The closer you are to the sky, the closer
you are to God*, said the guidebook.

The greenery sprouting from the rock's
phallic shape looked like moss invading

a lighthouse. The seats around us were
empty. Early morning lights pierced

the restaurant windows. A group of old
tourists in hats waited outside

for the first bus to take them up,
most of them with a camera in hand or hanging

around the neck. What I ordered that day,
I've long forgotten, but I recall my mother

in her sweater and her red scarf, a glass
of red wine beside her as she read the rundown

for next week's conference. The waiter
brought us a loaf of neatly sliced bread,

a block of butter, and an olive oil dip:
black spots in the plate's yellow pool.

Each of us munched on a slice of bread,
then our meals arrived—mother probably

ordered baked salmon or salad. Not wanting
to waste anything, she took several

napkins and rolled the rest of the bread.
She grew up not having enough and passed down

the same habit of not wasting food, although
most of the food she saved ended up moldy

anyway. Our fridge to this day full of leftovers
from days and sometimes weeks before.

When the waiter arrived with our check,
mother realized we were charged

fifty cents for each slice of bread we took.

Swamp

On Sunday nights, my mother tends to dream
of a little angel growing its wings
from a single stalk. Like the Pharaoh, she

searches the land to interpret her dream.
Her tears at her daughter's funeral float
our raft through the swamp. In her prayers, my

mother mentions her children one by one
as though trying to bargain with pity,
hoping she will get back the child she sold.

I want to guide my mother home—through riots,
hospital corridors, immigration
gates. When we arrive, Grandma's Chinese tea,

biscuits, and starfruits will be waiting with
the calmness of someone who lost her child.

Ode to the Activists

The highest career of an activist is not a position, but death. —Munir Said Thalib

The history books will remember you
    as traitors to your people and country,
        the few birds who broke formation and flew
from the flock, nested on a burning tree.

You cling to the past, eternal mourners,
    until the land becomes flooded anew,
        until the rivers are cleansed from red sins,
and all the island's holy warriors
    let the souls of their victims cross through.

You fight a losing battle every time:
    nothing but your skin as armor against
        batons, swung by those who deny war crimes.
Yet you march to your slaughter, without rest.

You cling to the future, hoping for rain,
    for any signs of change in this sorrow,
        this man-made drought, our eternal summer.
One swing of the scythe and you fall, as grain
    fields fall: to make bread for us tomorrow.

Sestina

For the umpteenth time, the mother
sits in the living room in silence—
eyes closed, lips as though reciting a prayer.
Perhaps she's asking for guidance
amid a storm hidden from others.
How to carry a grief that is timeless?

Her love for the departed is timeless.
During the day she's a teacher, at night, a mother
to three children who yell at each other.
This is a house that knows no silence,
a home to a parent who's too tired to give guidance.
Yet before each daybreak, she sits in prayer.

Not a day goes by without prayer,
her devotion to God remains timeless.
She's always listening for divine guidance,
anything that can console a mother.
Her heart grieves in silence,
because she has learned to never burden others.

Ever since she was a child, she has been an *other*:
the kids at Sunday school mocked her incoherent prayers,
her college friends made fun of her in silence—
her loneliness a ghost, timeless.
Even when she was about to become a mother
no one gave her any guidance.

Even without any guidance
she has never asked help from others.
Even before she was a mother
she has always been a prayer.
Her heart's too broad and timeless
to be kept alone and in silence.

After her daughter's casket was closed, she preferred silence.
No one knew how to console or dared to give guidance,
now that she was carrying something timeless.
Her friends, neighbors, they disappeared among the others.
She talked with her only comforter through prayer.
Once, I heard the soft words of my mother.

The silence in this house is unlike any other.
Yes, there's peace in seeking guidance in prayer.
"Help me bear this pain that is timeless," says the mother.

Visitor

Even my birthplace
    was never my own—I live
        unwanted from the country before,

the country to come.
    This, too, is a burden that
        my father can't hide under the threads

of his shirt, like a
    lump people would call sin, or
        the wage of it. My mother mourns

in the only way
    most Indonesians know how:
        every day, every night in silence.

Someday, her grief will
    morph into a marble child.
        It will stand in the living room for

visitors to see.
    I know, I'm everything and
        nothing at once: the child who survived,

the child who shouldn't.
    Still, I carry a shadow
        on my shoulders when I cross between

continents. When I return,
    my mother shows me
        what she has done to the place: black drapes,

ceramic tiles, fake
    tulips, and a lump of stone
        beside the old piano, waiting

to be sculpted.

Altar

I carry mountains wherever I go—from the crater lake of Rinjani, the blue fires of Ijen, to the everlasting smoke of Merapi—I drag my feet in the dirt so the land remembers my footsteps, a path for the ghosts of my ancestors to follow. But this is not the childhood Grandma once tried to run from: bullet casings under her feet on streets full of collapsed rooftops, men with torches and bamboo spears declaring a new era. They were singing they don't want my kind here, they don't want me, me, unborn and afraid—wait. This is someone else's story. This is not my land anymore, this is not me, I should never have left my childhood. Look, mother can barely walk, she asks for tea, asks for biscuits, calls my name in her sleep, but I'm nowhere to be found—even the songbirds have stopped their chorus, blaming me for forgetting the mountains. I think of a future when I can start over, but in that future, I still drag my feet, to the shore.

II

Sometimes we are like birds thudding into windows

—Tess Liem

City of Flood

/

Morning seems like night.
How long has it been raining?
I walk down the stairs

to find an unwelcomed guest:
a pool of muddied
water, claiming the living

room. As I wade to
the front door, the lukewarm pool
soaks my pants, thighs, and

underwear. Mud splashes my
t-shirt. I open
the door—a current of leaves,

sticks, and plastic bags
swarms inside. Outside, all I
can glimpse is water.

My scooter stands stupidly
by the metal fence,
rendered useless. The driveway,

the street, the garden—
they're the same now. Just like that,
society ceases

its operations. I try
to call my parents
but there's no service. Power

has always been first
to go out, electrical
current releasing

everywhere. Go to higher
ground and find others,
I think. Find dryness amid

this city of flood.

//

Even if this would all go away, will the water forget what we have done, what we continue to do? Every year, the rain, the tide, the flood. Yet, when it is dry, we refuse to believe in the prophecy, the prophecy that is a warning, a cycle. Someday, the whole ocean will empty itself and we must receive.

I try to wade across the city, to my family. Each step takes a full motion from my body. The closer to the center, the deeper the water. It's up to my elbows now. Someone in a raincoat is sharing their bread with the group. Another one is passing bottled water. Children laugh as they wrestle each other in the water. A truck speeds through, splashing everyone.

Lifeboats in the distance. I greet the volunteers. An elder with no teeth smiles at me. I nod my head slightly. The boat takes me to the nearest shelter. I remember I haven't eaten since last night. Inside the church at Jalan Kayu Putih, I see refugees sitting and sleeping on floor mats. I look for a familiar face and find no one. A church member arrives with rice boxes. I help her distribute them among the evacuees. I take my portion, sit in the corner. I pray for the rain to stop.

/

Where there is life, there is a cycle.
We exist in this sequence,

both as disruptor and disrupted,
always in need of saving

and forsaking. There is time to wear
boots and time to run barefoot.

There is a time to repaint the walls
and time to leave the walls be.

There is time to break bread and pass it
around, and a time to fast.

There is a time to cry with the clouds,
and time to sing with the birds.

A time to curse, a time to forgive.
A time to love, and a time

to let go. Time to say everything
and a time to stay silent.

Now is time for the storm to run its course.

Dear Indonesia

Your

rivers

run bloody.

Your forests burn.

Your corals are stones.

You walk your streets as though

nothing is at stake, as though

no one was killed, as though there was

no massacre. I'm surprised I'm still

breathing. Death has been looking for me since

I was a child—like a mist—it does not stop

until it runs satisfied. Ancestors, where have

you gone? Father, I'm beginning to forget the words

you scream each night, each morning. Mother, what language did you raise me in, can you recall? My feet remain sore since I've left

you both, sore from all the running. Will the day come when I can show

my face to the darkness and not be afraid of what I see? When will

death stop following me? Indonesia, Indonesia, I'm tired. I'm here

and aware of all the dying. Death waits for me, has my name written on its

white palm. My body bleeds. My bones shatter. You hunger for your next sacrifice. I

want to forget everything, but so many walls stand in the night. They all stand whitely,

remind me of death's face. Let me forget you, Motherland, your spears, your torches, your floods, your

dryness, your streets, your forests, your mists, your graves, your names, your faces. Let me go, let me sleep.

Overflow

Outside the walls of Jakarta, the tide
        roars. A mosque stands amid the waters—
                like a lighthouse in the sea—only its golden
                        minaret remains dry.

        Inside the walls, the waves offer
                coral, algae, kelp, and kresek,
                      spread out on a concrete ditch.
Not far away, a man stands in the watery streets,

                submerges his hands, and waits
                      for a fish to swim close.
In the city that is never dry:
        volunteers wear life vests, children practice

            butterfly strokes in the canal, an inflatable raft
                filled with pregnant women exits a hospital,
                      and an old couple offers tea and coffee
from the window of their drowned house.

            A current of waste in the murky waters:
                plastic bags, rubber sandals, toys,
plastic cups—they claim the city
        as their own.

                Motherland, we, your children live
on borrowed time, the scraped off wall
        can't keep the water away anymore.
            When the whole ocean comes, where will we go?

Rafflesia

Some things you never know until a friend
tells you, like how ghost means owl in your words,
cockatoo means older sibling in his.

The sun is the eye of the day, a sea-
horse is forever a seahorse. Some words
we love, we'd kiss them, and others? We wish

they were wrapped with an embalmed animal
skin. How quickly a harmless joke can turn
into rotting flesh, a headless cow

that follows me to sleep. Soon, carrion
insects claim my bed as their feeding ground.
When it comes to quiet remarks about

our women's seductive, slender thighs, one
of us won't forget. Whether my friend meant
it as a compliment does not erase

his footsteps. When he says *I want to lose
myself between her thighs*, he's pointing to
that woman over there, whose ancestors

arrived in the same boat as mine, who brought
the same foreign gods of dirt and fortune.

Cina Komunis

If only you, my friend, see me

      as the water rooster
          I am, and not a well for you

to throw bodies into. The gods

      of my ancestors drowned
    on their way here, swept

by the tide, their remains

      scattered like their worshippers.
    I am a forever lost,

these dead gods, I carry wherever I go.

      The government sells our
    land, exports our workers

for cheap. Still, you blame

      the ghosts of my dead, the Chinese
        Communists, forgetting the masses

have murdered them all.

Flood Ghazal

Raindrops knock on my roof, they cry like a child in the flood.
Tonight, I'm terrified. My mind wanders wild in the flood.

Like a snake, the waters slither and slide through the house gates.
I dream I was the only one who survived in the flood.

Help me! I cry. The waters carry my voice through the swamp.
Who can hear me? Can a body be revived in the flood?

Take me with you. Hold my hand as we wade the waters.
I can't walk alone as though I was exiled in the flood.

Am I dreaming or am I not used to all the water?
As a lonely child, I wished to be baptized in the flood.

Please, stay. Don't let me go. Don't abandon me to the rain.
When you left, I said I was alright. I lied in the flood.

Men shouldn't cry, so people say, and I was named after
a wise man: Sophronius. I'm a fool. I cry in the flood.

Ganyang Cina

I have found my kind hiding within
the walls of their shophouses. They speak in
a forbidden language among their own,
one which I've never learned. They've changed their names

into something easier to pronounce:
a forest is shaped into a *monk*, a
memory is molded into *faith* and
the *flood* dries up and becomes *sky*. Some have

abandoned history but still believe
the golden cat brings fortune, number four
means a bad omen, flipping a steamed fish
will destroy your wealth. The elders believe

in less likely things: like a race riot,
those carrying signs demanding our heads.

Cina

ci·na /ˈtʃɪnə / *offensive* 1. He said he would protect me should the mob come: // "hundreds of incensed demonstrators / ran from the scene yelling / 'kill *cina*' and brandishing weapons." 2. Those who try to pass as the kind they're not: // grandmother was pregnant when the police escorted her and her four children to change their legal name. 3. The sacrificed: // "the crowd rampaged / through the city, pulling *cina* / off pedicabs and motor scooters, / hacking them with long knives, / ransacking their stalls in the central market, / killing or wounding all who resisted." 4. When I miss my childhood friend, I try to remember him singing *cina* songs, the songs he pretended to know the lyrics to.

In the Waves of Midnight

I have witnessed my kind
migrating through salt and water.

They hurled their sacks of clothes
from the boat to the shore.

From wood to embers, and from ashes
to homes, mothers kept past lives in their pockets.

I have listened to Grandma's bedtime stories
turning into a grocery list.

    There once was a pastor

I have passed down the family fables
to my younger cousins, to my many nephews and nieces.

    who ran away to become a farmer.

Lavender has grown into an adolescent,
a burning flame into a silent daughter.

    He planted cucumbers, lettuce,

I have kissed the earth out of loneliness—
dirt, snow, loneliness, and mooncakes

    milk, and Dutch biscuits...

taste the same. I have fallen in love
with a stranger on the mountain,

    Here, our ancestors held out their baskets

knowing we'll never see each other again.
I have roamed the lands to find my grave.

    as they baked their dough under the sun

Here, I have baptized myself shirtless
in the waves of midnight,

    and days grew to months, months to decades.

as the water fills my mouth,
I can see the ashes rising to life.

III

Pada akhirnya
Kita pun pasrah – karena
Tidak bisa mengusir
Bayang-bayang kita sendiri

—Rita Oetoro

City of Concrete

Echoes of the past: streets named after swamps, mango trees perfume neighborhoods, watery rose apples in a puddle, a lizard drinks out of a plastic cup, a snake sleeps on a porch, bats decorate the gray sky, a chorus of frogs singing in the sewers.

This morning, engines rule: buses packed with office workers, sedans driven by chauffeurs on their way to drop children at schools, motorcycles winding through a sea of metal and rust. In this city, people seldom walk in daylight—the air invaded by gas, smoke, and dust. Plastics and leftover rice litter the sidewalk. Garbage cans overflowing, a hunting ground for stray cats and rats.

The masses come out at night, when the rubbish and pollution remain veiled in the dark. The food stalls set up their folding tables at dusk, serving fried rice, meatballs, satays. Strangers eat together, share cigarettes, and sip sweet tea between curses as they talk shit about the government.

>The night belongs
>to us, the day,
>the rulers.

Dutch East Indies

When Indonesia was not yet Indonesia,
seafarers hauling white sails arrived on our shores.
They brought their white ideas
of what it means to be a civilization.

Seafarers hauling white sails arrived on our shores,
traded nutmegs, mace, cloves,
and what it means to be a civilization.
They built outposts and colonial houses,

traded nutmeg, mace, and cloves,
brought teachers, missionaries, and soldiers.
They built outposts and colonial houses,
claimed island after island.

Their teachers, missionaries, and soldiers
lived with the *pribumi* but at the top of a caste system
they had forced on island after island.
Our hospitality translated as weakness,

the *pribumi* lived at the bottom of a caste system.
Now the sails, bayonets, and walls are gone,
but our hospitality was translated as weakness.
Still their white ideas flow

strong as sails, bayonets, and walls.
Unseen among us,
their white ideas still flow:
the foundation of our civilization.

Unseen among us,
they brought their white ideas,

the foundation of our civilization—
when Indonesia was not yet Indonesia.

Chinezenmoord

Children carry the warm river water
      in wooden buckets, portion by portion

                        until the river turns haunted. *Bodies*
                            float like glass bottles, says a witness.

      The children scream, quiver. They run home
empty-handed, their smallness shrinking them?

                        No water means no meal for the family.
                    No river, no water. *Headless*. The Dutch

soldiers offer two gold coins for each
      Chinese head laid at their feet. They check the eyes:

                      do they curve like ripe mangoes? Does the skin
                          share the same color as fruit flesh? This is

how to start the wheel of genocide. Hang
      the old and the sick in front of City Hall.

                                        They deserve it for taking over our
                                country. Give us enough time and the wheel

repeats. My kind has no land to begin
        with, only a field of red to empty ourselves into.

                                        People forget, but the concrete roads can't,
                                                what has been spilled here before. And

the river remembers: how we die
        is never up to us—our bodies ripen

                                        for the taking.

Where a Name Is Buried

for Lee Siok Lie

If your gaze were the fleeting
       crimson of dusk,

              I would be the fool
              chasing that dying

                     light, hoping I could follow you

into an everlasting morning.
       I never called

              all the years I was away.
              Through clouded nights

                     and flooded mind, I remained
breathing, beating without you.

I know, I'm only a child
       running away

              from a growing shadow. It's no
       use. I never called, not because

              I didn't care,
you raised me this way:

       a gladiola to be watered, obedient

to the shifting of light and dark.

    You told me not to call you

          by your real name.
          I grew up not knowing

              the faint spark hidden
        behind its meaning. When Grandma died,

you didn't cry, not even
        when your siblings took turns

to pour cologne and scatter lilies
      over her body, not even when they

         shut the casket. Your mother
         buried her secret name,

             but perhaps you don't have to.

Ancestral Burden

I wasn't one of the thousands of Chinese killed in 1740.
I wasn't one of the thousands of Chinese forced
to pledge allegiance or shot by the Japanese army.

I wasn't one of the thousands of Chinese whose houses burned
in the War of Independence. I wasn't one of the thousands of
Chinese killed in 1965. I wasn't one of the thousands of Chinese

whose stores burned in 1998. I wasn't one of the thousands
of Chinese whose sons and daughters were killed—or worse.
I wasn't one of the sons. I wasn't one of the daughters.

I wasn't one of them. Today, I breathe slowly. I'm thankful for this
land. Living remains the living's burden. Let the past be the past.
What has happened, has happened. I'm thankful for this body.

IV

相见时难别亦难
(It's hard to see you and when I see you it's hard to leave you)
—Li Shangyin

City of Smoke

September 26, 2019: Jakarta police fire tear gas amid unrest over conservative reforms.

    Thick smoke conceals the red sky.
                Tires burn in the streets.

                                              every act of abortion is
                                          punishable by imprisonment

Roadblocks on the highway exits. Armored
        carriers unload troops in heavy boots.
                Tear gas explodes, right outside your office.

                                          anyone who commits blasphemy
                                            will be jailed for five years

            Dinda, how will you get home today?
    How safe are the streets? The air you
        have to breathe?

This city, my home,
        now a city of smoke.

                                                anyone who promotes sex
                                              education will be fined

            Those who could leave
have already left. I left long before
        anyone threw the first stone.

Don't worry, you texted me.
      I wish I could hold you,
but can only take the shirt you packed for me
      before I left.

I raise it to my nose:
    lavender and sweat.

              anyone who lives together like a husband and wife
                 outside of marriage will be jailed or fined

    Will they take me away
      if I return?

                And what would I return to?
                A city, a cemetery?

Explosions in the streets. Wet bodies against batons and shields.
    A police car runs over a pedestrian.
   Another tree burns down
      all the way to the roots.

Missing

There lies a cold and soundless space between
us, like manna left untouched at night.
      Come morning, I no longer find you here.
I wait in bed, drift with my thoughts where
the waves of doubt take me. Underwater
rests a shipwreck of memories. How
long must we gaze at this uncertainty?
      If you won't return tomorrow, please
      take this heart that you alone have cracked. To be
empty is all I seek—no sound, no beat—
anything to stop this ache on repeat.
      Let me live my days alone in peace.
      And don't look back. Go live and be complete.

Notations on Letting Go

                                            1. e4

I taught you this
    opening on what

I knew would be
    our last day. Many
                                    e5.

ways we could have
    done this: developed

our pieces, fought
    for the center, or
                       2.f4

kept holding to
    what was between us.

Like a young knight
    pretending to know
                                 exf4.

the field, I said
    the route was easy,

but I was as
    lost as a hanging
                       3.Nf3

pawn. *What now?* you
    asked. If it were up

to me, I'd say:
    let go. Retreat to

your familiar
    territory, your

king. Yes, I was
    the one who had to
move.

Love & Sambal

Without the lingering of your redness,
    my tongue would be so lonely for pain.
   What am I if not a masochist?
Instead of a kiss, I ask for the same
   thing each time, a momentary bliss.

Perhaps I've never been allowed to love
    in the ways I wanted: undisturbed,
   slow, without the world at my doorstep.
I too, have stopped asking for anything
   other than my share. My burden.

I turn to you then, sambal, for I know
    your familiar burn, always pleasant.
   Your body: a crimson grind, soft skin
of a dried pepper, sprinkled with a taste
   of lime—watery. Yes, I ask for all this.

Aftertaste

I can hardly keep my food down. The last
   meal that didn't taste bitter was the mutton soup
mother had prepared the night before I left.
   What's the opposite of digestion? What to call

      a hunger so great you try to cradle it to sleep?
Every morning is like a hangover, warm fluids
   tickling the insides of my cheeks. I can only
blame food poisoning for so long before

the food starts blaming the body. No, I'm not
   sick, I just don't like staring across an empty seat,
the humming of fans, and the clank my spoon makes
   every time it touches the plate. One meal a day

      is more than enough for this belly.
Let me rephrase my thoughts.
   Things my body can't stand: fish heads floating
on a pool of thick, brown soup, the pungent aroma

of bread, and your mother—the physician—
   yelling at you for loving someone like me.
Things I love: steaming hot noodles with *bakso* on top,
   eggs over rice for breakfast, rum and raisin ice cream

      (or just rum), and of course, you, the sigh you let
out when we embrace after months, your waiting.
   What I miss the most? The aftertaste
of sharing a dessert with you.

Reflections of a Failed Chinese Lover

             When I saw the picture of you

together at the park,

      two entangled swans by the lake,

   I noticed the hearts and wishes from your friends,

                the
blessings

     that eluded me for seven years.

It was his skin, I figured,

              perfectly matched

         with yours.

     My body was a forbidden song,

a tune you could only

          hum in the dark.

Reminiscence

I no longer remember the night
I proposed to you: what you wore,
where we went, what you ordered—
am I a bad person?

Not unlike a moldy photo,
my memory of us, too, gets a little blurry
with each day passing by
after you left.

Exhausted and defeated,
I retreat to that unremembered night,
as well as the many nights that never unfolded,
and I pretend I'm there again.

I redecorate our first apartment,
the one we were planning to buy
(but never got to), with a painting
of tulips, your favorite (or was it lavender?).

I wait for you to come home,
in my favorite chair, reading poetry I enjoy.
After three books or so, I start to fear

you got lost on your way here.

I Rest My Mother Tongue

I rest my mother tongue, let her sleep
in my mouth. Nine months have passed without
a childhood word leaving me. Slowly,

I forget street names, my family's
last meal together, and those who made
me smile. Words depart—my lexicon,

an incomplete jigsaw puzzle, full
of dust. Do I exist only for
one language? Can't my body contain

a memory without forgetting
another? In my aloneness, I
adjust to silence, not unlike eyes

in the darkness. I'm thinking of you,
Dinda, and what language it was you
first spoke to me. It doesn't matter.

I'm here and you are so far away.
I hope I haven't lost too much of
myself when we meet again. Which

is better: to write or to be written?

Monsoon Elegy

I'm thinking about the ways I could've said goodbye
properly. No, not with a text, half-written at four
in the morning, after drowning the night alone

with whisky, next to unfolded clothes on the bed.
Nor with a call, just barely a ring before hanging
up and convincing the mind enough was enough.

Maybe I could've said it a week earlier—
before passing through the immigration officers,
when we were at the lounge filled with unpatronized,

expensive restaurants at midnight, after not
having slept at all, like the dozens of flights before.
I'm not sure which of what I did was worse; saying

I needed a break, knowing what was to come, or
the words after the silence was broken. *Even if
we were to get married, I would still be depressed.*

The damage done. Seven years of fighting against
your parents, my siblings, our friends, and the world. We were
too busy draining the waters from our boat, we

couldn't see the direction our sail was heading.
We grew up unallied, no one but each other to
show us the way. When I jumped overboard, the storm

you feared was endless, began to quiet—it was
almost biblical: I gave myself to the waters
so you could return home. And the tide swallowed this

body. Amid my unending sea, I prayed for
your happiness. Now my prayers are answered. After
the monsoon, the flood will cease, the road will clear. What

remains is dirt for me to clean. I understand
what happened, had to happen. Nothing I could've done
could change what was to come. Perhaps the world wasn't

ready. Perhaps it will never be.

Coda: Present Day

The belief in the almighty God.

Just and civilized humanity.

The unity of Indonesia.

Democracy under the wise guidance of representative consultations.

Social justice for the people of Indonesia.

　　—*"Pancasila," the five foundational principles of Indonesia.*

Friends, welcome! Are you connected? Are you
bearing witness? Everything's happening
without us! Here, take a slice of this pie.
How goes the war? How goes the invasion?

Don't ask where the cake is. Our leaders bought
too many guns and not enough desserts.
Metal blades in the sky! Sky songs for us
all to hear. How goes the conspiracy?

How do you win against hemorrhoids? How
do you win against capitalism?
How do you win against patriarchy?
This is getting too therapy-esque—here's

a pill to make you sleep. Here's another.
For God's sake, stop questioning the system.

> Do Indonesia's Abusive 'Virginity
> Tests' Hurt UN Peacekeeping Operations?
> —Human Rights Watch

> Indonesia Second Least Literate of 61 Nations
> —Central Connecticut State University

> Fake news about communism in
> Indonesia blamed for triggering riot
> in Jakarta
> —The *Sydney Morning Herald*

For God's sake, stop questioning the system;
it's here to stay, the heart of existence

without which we would remain dry and parched.
I've filled my silvered cup with water but
I keep forgetting to drink. Don't forget
to drink! The sun forgot once and look what

happened to it. I keep filling my cup
with water but it turns to blood before
I can even take a sip. Everyone
keeps telling me to drink. They sense my thirst;

I've emptied a well and still I'm not quenched.
The wealthy are laughing, the poor singing.
Everyone is writing about sex! Why
have I been writing only about death?

Indonesia: Stop Intimidating
Participants in Events Concerning
1965 Human Rights Violations
—Amnesty International

Twenty years on, victims of 1998
Indonesia violence still seek justice
—Reuters

Palm oil 'decimating' wildlife in
Malaysia and Indonesia, solutions
elusive
—The *Straits Times*

Have we been talking only about death?
Have I died more than I have lived? I will
plant a heart in the desert. I'm stitching

this body back whole, replacing my heart
with a towel. Aren't I soft? I'm running
out of threads to give. Burgers for sale, gem

stones for sale, birth charts for sale, tote bags, skin
care, hair products, leather shoes, guns, pink pills—
everything's for sale. The villages on

the mountains in Java are for sale. Clouds
for sale. My heart's for sale. I'm probably
worth two dozen chickens all packed in one

coop, and maybe throw in a cow or two.
Stitch by stitch I'm completing this body.

Indonesia: Indigenous Peoples
Losing Their Forests
—Human Rights Watch

Huge Oil Spill in Land of Earthquakes,
Tsunamis and Volcanoes
—*The New York Times*

Area burned in Indonesia fires
'greater than the Netherlands'
—Al Jazeera

Stitch by stitch I'm completing this body:
my jawline stretched, my shoulders broadened, yes

to longer legs and yes to more chest hair!
I should now have a better chance to survive
in the apocalypse. I no longer

recognize my face in the river. All
I've ever wanted was to love and be
loved in return without having to fight

a whole (fucking) system. Why can't I live
without having to justify my worth?
I've played out all my possibilities:

not a day will pass where I'll be enough.
No matter how much I change my body,
there's no future where I won't be lonely.

> Indonesia earthquake: Hundreds
> dead in Palu quake and tsunami
> —BBC

> Ash Fills the Sky As Bali's Mount
> Agung Erupts
> —NPR

> Sunda Strait tsunami death toll hits
> 429, Navy discovers bodies at sea
> —*The Jakarta Post*

There's no future where I won't be lonely.
I keep checking my phone every minute
even though no one ever looks for me.
Love is an eel—it keeps slipping from my
hands, even when I hold with all my might.
Some nights, I forget my name, after not

hearing it for so long. Please don't worry,
I'm in therapy! Everything's peachy
and sweet. If only life was as short as
a man's penis, then I wouldn't have the time
to worry about a lonesome future.
In the next life, I'll be hunting eels in

the muddy sewers of my neighborhood:
a glimpse of the apocalypse to come.

Papua protests: Racist taunts open
deep wounds
—BBC

Black Lives Matter protests spark
reminder of 'deeply rooted' racial
injustice towards West Papuans
—ABC News

Seven Papuan activists convicted of
treason after anti-racism protests
—*The Guardian*

A glimpse of the apocalypse to come:
cadavers in the streets, bodies of those

who looked different than the majority,
the sky full of smoke, no bird songs, just noise
of guns echoing the night walls. Look, these
streets of flood, neighborhoods of missing names,
cities of forgotten sins—they all make
this land that we pollute and call country.

People in power will do anything
to keep their hands heavy with stolen dirt.
I'm masturbating to the idea
that someday we'll live in a world where we
won't cause only destruction. People, look:
our arms raised up, we're embracing the flames.

Indonesia: Papuan protesters shot,
beaten and racially abused by
security forces—new research
                —Amnesty International

'We are living in a war zone': violence
flares in West Papua as villagers forced
to flee
                —*The Guardian*

United Nations refuses to accept West
Papua independence petition, says it
will not 'do anything against Indonesia'
                —South China *Morning Post*

Raise your arms, embrace and dance with the flames.
Friends, the heat will cradle your loneliness

if you let it! Global warming, rising sea
levels, and the dying ecosystem
will make you forget your daily problems!
None of us will matter eventually.

Human rights violations? What are you
talking about? We'll be dead anyway!

The wrath of God will come. The cause of wrath:
we've forgotten to love one another
and instead use religion as a license
to discriminate and kill. All of this

has happened before—haven't we tired
the history books enough? Why can't we change?

Victims of 1998 Indonesia riots
still silent-report
                                            —Reuters

New Report Says Official Denials
of Indonesian Rapes Hinder
Investigation
                                —Human Rights Watch

Indonesian police shaved
transgender women and made them
dress as men
                                            —CNN

Why can't we change the course of history?
Aren't we all tired of the amnesia

in our collective memory? Why do
we let hate dictate the course of our state?
Why are we bound to walk in the morning
with our heart corrupted by anger? Why

do the rotten words of those in power
have stronghold in our mind? Aren't we better

than this? Aren't we better than those who came
before us? Did our ancestors not live
hand-in-hand before nationalism?
Before imperialism? Before

colonialism? Before belief?
My God, what have your lost people become?

> Two men publicly caned 77 times
> for having sex in Indonesia
> —NBC News

> Indonesia proposes bill to force
> LGBTQ people into 'rehabilitation'
> —NBC News

> Indonesia massacres: Declassified
> US files shed new light
> —BBC

God, look how lost your people have become.
In worshipping you, I have lost my faith.
I no longer believe in the preacher

and his words. The scholar and his verses.
The teacher and his lessons. The leader
and his promise. The butcher and his meat.
I see through the fog of hatred and lies,

no matter how well-packaged they might be,
hidden under the guise of religion.
Hate is hate. Hate defiles the pure heart, like

pouring concrete over a well. When dark
times come, it's easy to pass the blame on
some other group that we don't know or care.
We forget those who share our motherland.

A Dangerous Place for Indonesian Women
—*The ASEAN Post*

Consent vs 'nikah': Indonesia's culture war won't end anytime soon
—*The Jakarta Post*

Indonesia's culture wars overly fixated on sex
—*Asian Times*

We forget those who share our motherland.
No one is born a demon, but many
remain demonized. We let one-sided
narratives control how we perceive

each other. Even the migratory
birds cross oceans, borders, the hemisphere. How
often do we step to the other

side before othering people who share
this earth with us? Don't we all come from one breath?
While we have the most means of connection,
we remain more disconnected than ever.

Despite having a body, we don't care
for other bodies. Everything means what?
Nothing. We all have become nothing.

Sexual Violence on Indonesian
Campuses Is a Critical Emergency
—*Jakarta Globe*

He Raped 13 Girls, Impregnating
Several of Them. He Was Their
Teacher.
—VICE

'They laughed in my face': Riau
student says university brushed off
sexual assault report
—*The Jakarta Post*

Everything means nothing to everyone.
I'm doing my best in society

by staying invisible, like any
good minority. I keep my head bowed down.

I stay quiet in the corner, remain
unspoken unless I'm spoken to first.

When someone asks, "How are you?" I shut up.
I don't talk about the extinct tigers,

the small elephants losing their forests,
the corals turning lifeless, into stones.

Instead, I say, "I'm doing fine, thank you."
And I ask, "How are you? How goes the war?"

Friends, do you too, pity the nonhumans:
the worms, the sparrows, the orangutans?

Churches attacked and one man
killed in clashes in Aceh, Indonesia
—BBC

Burning temples, organised violence:
Will Indonesia ever be tolerant?
—*Asean Today*

In Indonesia, Chinese Deity Is
Covered in Sheet
—*The New York Times*

The worms, the sparrows, the orangutans.
The earth, the sky, the sea.

The flood, the earthquake, the tsunami.
The mind, the soul, the body.

God, creations, the story.
The day, the night, the dreams.

The roots, the tree, the leaves.
The sun, the moon, the stars.

The prayer, the ritual, the belief.
The preacher, the worshipper, the thief.

The love, the mercy, the acceptance.
The peace, the harmony, the tranquility.

The people, the majority, the minority.
We forget what we see and do not see.

Chinese Indonesians in Jakarta fear attacks on the community, as anti-China hoaxes spread
—South China *Morning Post*

Rising Anti-Chinese Sentiment in Indonesia
—*The Asean Post*

In Jakarta, Reports of Numerous Rapes of Chinese in Riots
—*The New York Times*

We forget what we see and do not see.
We disregard our nation's history.
We keep chanting our national motto,
unity in diversity, but

we keep our prejudice. We stop using
plastic straws and say, *we have done enough*.
We watch a documentary and say,
we have done enough. We go to protests
and say, *we have done enough*. Have we done

anything? The poor remain poor. The rich
remain rich. The dead remain dead. What has
changed? Other than we've gotten older and
that we've gotten desensitized to all
the cruelty going on, what has changed?

Indonesia haze causes sky to turn
blood red
         —BBC

Indonesia is burning. So why is the
world looking away?
       —*The Guardian*

Jakarta, the fastest-sinking city
in the world
         —BBC

The cruelty goes on, but what has changed?
We live in the system, the system that
has devoured our people, the system
we worship. O motherland, you remain

beautiful and free. We are your children.
Forgive us, we have failed you. We don't know
how to live without desecrating you,
without destroying trees for palm oil,
without destroying the soil for roads,

without polluting the sky for our bread.
We live, but know not how to let live. We
eat, but know not how to feed the hungry.
We sleep, but know not how to let you rest.
Friends, we're at the end. Are you connected?

A watery onslaught from sea, sky and land
in the world's fastest-sinking city
—Mongabay

'Running out of time': Indonesia
struggles to kick coal addiction
—*The Jakarta Post*

Time running out for witnesses
of Indonesia's darkest hour
—BBC

For our sake, stop questioning the system!
So what if we only talk about death?
Stitch by stitch we're completing our bodies.
There's no future where we won't be lonely.
A glimpse of the apocalypse to come:
our arms raised up, we're embracing the flames.
Why can't we change the course of history?

God, look how lost your people have become.
We forget those who share our motherland.
Nothing. We all have become nothing.
The worms, the sparrows, the orangutans:
we forget what we see and do not see.
The cruelty goes on, but what has changed?
Friends, we're at the end. Are you connected?

Notes

The section I epigraph from Li-Young Lee comes from "The Cleaving" in *The City in Which I Love You* (BOA Editions, 1990).

p. 9: The title refers to "Surat Bukti Kewarganegaraan Republik Indonesia" or "SBKRI" (Republic of Indonesia Certificate of Citizenship), which was an identity card denoting citizenship to the country. This "proof" of citizenship was required to enter academia, obtain a passport, register to vote, and get married. Only non-native Indonesians were required to have SBKRI, primarily the Chinese-Indonesians.

p. 14: The title refers to the May 1998 riots of Indonesia, which were primarily fueled against Chinese-Indonesians. The waves of the riots lasted throughout the year.

p. 19: Munir Said Thalib was an Indonesian lawyer and human rights activist. He was assassinated on September 7, 2004.

The section II epigraph from Tess Liem comes from *Obits* (Coach House Books, 2018).

p. 28: The italicized lines are adapted from Natalie Diaz's poem, "The First Water Is the Body" found in *Postcolonial Love Poem* (Graywolf Press, 2020).

p. 32: "Kresek" is an Indonesian word for plastic bags. The poem lists the kinds of waste found during a typical flood in Jakarta, based on Shuker et al: "Indonesia—Marine debris hotspot rapid assessment: synthesis report." The World Bank, 2018.

p. 33: The title comes from one of the national flowers of Indonesia, *Rafflesia arnoldii*. Also known as "corpse flower," the flower has a lifespan of merely one week, when it attracts carrion insects.

p. 36: The title loosely translates as "Hang the Chinese." The phrase is a commonly put on protest signs against Chinese-Indonesians.

p. 37: The quotations come from Tsai, Yen-ling and Douglas Kammen. "Chapter 6: Anti-communist Violence and the Ethnic Chinese in Medan, North Sumatra." *The Contours of Mass Violence in Indonesia*, 1965-1968, edited by Douglas Kammen and Katherine McGregor, NUS Press, 2012, pp. 131-155.

The section III epigraph from Rita Oetoro comes from *Tonggak 3* (Gramedia, 1987).

p. 44: Dutch East Indies was the Dutch colonial name for Indonesia when the archipelago was still under the occupation of the Vereenigde Oostindische Compagnie (VOC) and the Dutch government. "Pribumi" translates to "natives"; the word is a replacement for the Dutch colonial term, "inlander."

p. 46: The title comes from the Dutch word, which translates to "The Murder of Chinese"; it refers to the 1740 Batavia massacre, where around 10,000 ethnic Chinese were slaughtered. Also known as "Geger Pacinan" or "Tragedi Angke" in Indonesian.

p. 48: "Lee Siok Lie" is my mother's birth Chinese name, which she had to change because of 127/U/Kep/12/1966, one of the many anti-Chinese legislations issued by Suharto's New Order regime.

The section IV epigraph is from Li Shangyin (李商隐), a Chinese poet of the late Tang Dynasty. The translation is by Jingrun Lin, used with permission.

About the Author

Jeddie Sophronius is the author of the poetry collections *Happy Poems & Other Lies* (Codhill Press, 2024), *Interrogation Records* (Gaudy Boy, 2024), and the chapbook *Blood·Letting* (Quarterly West, 2023). A Chinese-Indonesian writer from Jakarta, they received their MFA from the University of Virginia, where they currently serve as a lecturer in English. The recipient of the 2023 Gaudy Boy Poetry Book Prize, their poems have appeared in *The Cincinnati Review*, *The Iowa Review*, *Prairie Schooner*, and elsewhere. Read more of their work at nakedcentaur.com.

About The Word Works

Since its founding in 1974, The Word Works has steadily published volumes of contemporary poetry and presented public programs. Its imprints include the Washington Prize, the Tenth Gate Prize, the Hilary Tham Capital Collection, and International Editions.

Monthly, The Word Works offers free programs in its Café Muse Literary Salon. Starting in 2023, the winners of the Jacklyn Potter Young Poets Competition will be presented in the June Café Muse program.

As a 501(c)3 organization, The Word Works has received awards from the National Endowment for the Arts, the National Endowment for the Humanities, the D.C. Commission on the Arts & Humanities, the Witter Bynner Foundation, Poets & Writers, The Writer's Center, Bell Atlantic, the David G. Taft Foundation, and others, including many generous private patrons.

An archive of artistic and administrative materials in the Washington Writing Archive is housed in the George Washington University Gelman Library. The Word Works is a member of the Community of Literary Magazines and Presses.

wordworksbooks.org

Other Word Works Books

Annik Adey-Babinski, *Okay Cool No Smoking Love Pony*
Karren L. Alenier, *Wandering on the Outside*
Emily August, *The Punishments Must Be a School*
Jennifer Barber, *The Sliding Boat Our Bodies Made*
Mary Block, *Love from the Outer Bands*
Andrea Carter Brown, *September 12*
Willa Carroll, *Nerve Chorus*
Grace Cavalieri, *Creature Comforts* / *The Long Game: Poems Selected & New*
Abby Chew, *A Bear Approaches from the Sky*
Nadia Colburn, *The High Shelf*
Henry Crawford, *Binary Planet*
Barbara Goldberg, *Berta Broadfoot and Pepin the Short* / *Breaking & Entering: New and Selected Poems*
Akua Lezli Hope, *Them Gone*
Michael Klein, *The Early Minutes of Without: Poems Selected & New*
Deborah Kuan, *Women on the Moon*
Frannie Lindsay, *If Mercy*
Elaine Magarrell, *The Madness of Chefs*
Chloe Martinez, *Ten Thousand Selves*
Marilyn McCabe, *Glass Factory*
JoAnne McFarland, *Identifying the Body*
Leslie McGrath, *Feminists Are Passing from Our Lives*
Kevin McLellan, *Ornitheology*
Ron Mohring, *The Boy Who Reads in the Trees*
A. Molotkov, *Future Symptoms*
Ann Pelletier, *Letter That Never*
W. T. Pfefferle, *My Coolest Shirt*
Ayaz Pirani, *Happy You Are Here*
Robert Sargent, *Aspects of a Southern Story* / *A Woman from Memphis*
Roger Smith, *Radiation Machine Gun Funk*
Julia Story, *Spinster for Hire*
Maria Terrone, *No Known Coordinates*
Barbara Ungar, *After Naming the Animals*
Cheryl Clark Vermeulen, *They Can Take It Out*
Julie Marie Wade, *Skirted*
Miles Waggener, *Superstition Freeway*
Fritz Ward, *Tsunami Diorama*
Camille-Yvette Welsch, *The Four Ugliest Children in Christendom*
Amber West, *Hen & God*
Maceo Whitaker, *Narco Farm*

www.ingramcontent.com/pod-product-compliance
Lightning Source LLC
Chambersburg PA
CBHW060926170426
43192CB00025B/2906